MEMORY

WALTER DE LA MARE

Memory

and

OTHER POEMS

NEW YORK
HENRY HOLT AND COMPANY

COPYRIGHT, 1938,
BY
WALTER DE LA MARE

PRINTED IN THE
UNITED STATES OF AMERICA

To

POPPY AND ROGER

NOTE

THE author's grateful thanks are due to the Editors of the following periodicals, in which many of the poems contained in this collection first appeared: the *Spectator*, the *London Mercury*, *Nash's Magazine*, the *Argosy*, the *Observer*, *John o' London's Weekly*, *Time and Tide*, *Night and Day*, the *Listener*, *Country Life*, *Good Housekeeping*, *The Year's Poetry*.

CONTENTS

MEMORY

A SUNDAY

A child in the Sabbath peace, there—
Down by the full-bosomed river;
Sun on the tide-way, flutter of wind,
Water-cluck,—*Ever . . . for ever . . .*

Time itself seemed to cease there—
The domed, hushed city behind me;
Home how distant! The morrow would come—
But here, no trouble could find me.

A respite, a solacing, deep as the sea,
Was mine. Will it come again? . . . Never? . . .
Shut in the Past is that Sabbath peace, there—
Down by the full-bosomed river.

A POT OF MUSK

A glance—and instantly the small meek flower
Whispered of what it had to childhood meant;
But kept the angel secret of that far hour
    Ere it had lost its scent.

BROTHER AND SISTER

A turn of head, that searching light,
And—was it fancy?—a faint sigh:
I know not what; there leapt the thought,
We are old, now—she and I.

Old, though those eager clear blue eyes,
And lines of laughter along the cheek,
Far less of time than time's despite
To one who loves her speak. . . .

Besides, those pale and smiling lips,
That once with beauty were content,
Now wisdom too have learned; and that
No clock can circumvent. . . .

Nor is this world of ours a toy
That woe should darken when bed-time nears;
Still memory-sweet its old decoy,
And—well, what use in tears? . . .

So limped the brittle argument;
Yet—had I Prospero's wizardry,
She should at once have back her youth,
Whatever chanced to me.

POLLIE

Pollie is a simpleton;
'Look!' she cries, 'that *lovely* swan!'
And, even before her transports cease,
   Adds, 'But I do love geese.'

When a lark wings up the sky,
She'll sit with lips ajar, then sigh—
For rapture; and the rapture o'er,
   Whisper, 'What's music *for*?'

Every lesson I allot,
As soon as learned is clean forgot.
'L-O-V . . . ?' I prompt.   And she
   Smiles, but I catch no 'E.'

It seems in her round head you come
As if to a secret vacuum;
Whence then the wonder, love and grace
   Shining in that small face?

THE IRREVOCABLE

Weep no more, thou weary one;
Tears—and so beloved a face!
Raindrops on a daybreak flower—
Token of cold midnight's grace—
No more radiant are than these.
Both of transient darkness tell;
And but one least beam of morning
   Either will dispel.

I thy midnight was. . . . Yet word,
Easy, innocent of guile,
Weeping eyes and childlike lips
   Have conjured to a smile.
All forgotten, all forgiven.
Why remorse, then? . . . Well I know
The few clear stars still mine in heaven
Never shall now as brightly show.

ABSALOM

Vain, proud, rebellious Prince, thy treacherous hair,
Though thirty centuries have come and gone,
Still in that bitter oak doth thee ensnare;
Rings on that broken-hearted, *Son, my son!* . . .

And though, with childhood's tragic gaze, I see
Thee—idol of Israel—helpless in the tree,
Thy dying eyes turned darkened from the Sun;
Yet, of all faces in far memory's shrine—
Paris, Adonis, pale Endymion—
   The loveliest still is thine.

IN A LIBRARY

Would—would that there were
A book on that shelf
To teach an old man
To teach himself!—

The joy of some scribe,
Brush in service to quill,
Who, with bird, flower, landscape,
Emblem and vision,
Loved his margins to fill.

Then might I sit,
By true learning beguiled,
Far into the night
Even with self reconciled.
Retrieving the wisdom
I lost, when a child.

IN DISGRACE

The fear-dulled eyes in the pallid face
Stared at the darkening window-pane;
Sullen, derided, in disgrace—
They watched night narrowing in again—
Far-away shoutings; a furtive wind
Which a keyhole had found; a star aloof;
A heart at war with a blunted mind;
   And a spout dripping rain from the roof.

Drip—drip . . . till the light is gone;
But a heart not so hard as a stone.

'UNHEARD MELODIES'

A minstrel came singing in the way;
  And the children,
  Nothing saying,
  Gathered round him,
  From their playing,
In a bower of the shadowy may.

He stood in a loop of the green;
  And his fingers
  On the wires
  Feigned their heart's deep,
  Hidden desires
For a country that never was seen.

Like moonbeams in forests of trees,
  Like brook water
  Dropping sweetness,
  Like the wild hare
  In her fleetness,
Like the wings of the honey-sucking bees;

He drew each pure heart with his skill;
  With his beauty,
  And his azure,

And his topaz,
Gold for pleasure,
And his locks wet with dew of April.

Time sped; and night's shadows grew deep,
Came owl-hoot
From the thicket,
And the shrill note
Of the cricket
Called the children to silence and sleep. . . .

Strange, strange! though the minstrel is gone,
Yet that hawthorn
Fair and lonely
Stoops mutely
Waiting only
Till the clamour of noonday is done—

Until, in the faint skies of eve,
Far and sweetly,
Like a river,
Silver wires seem
Throbbing ever
As if echo in sorrow would grieve

In ears dulled with wrath and rebuke;
And like snowdrops
After winter,

Tired feet pause there,
And then enter
That bower by the midsummer brook.

O minstrel, keep thy tryst, sound thine airs
In a heart that
Oft forgets thee,
Scorns, reviles thee,
Tires, and frets thee
With the burden of silence it bears.

A CHILD ASLEEP

Angel of Words, in vain I have striven with thee,
Nor plead a lifetime's love and loyalty;
Only, with envy, bid thee watch this face,
    That says so much, so flawlessly,
        And in how small a space!

RESERVED

. . . 'I was thinking, Mother, of that poor old horse
   They killed the other day;
Nannie *says* it was only a bag of bones,
   But I hated it taken away.'
'Of course, sweet; but now the baker's man
Will soon have a nice new motor van.'

'Yes, Mother.   But when on our walk a squirrel
   Crept up to my thumb to be fed,
She shoo'd it away with her gloves—like this!
   They ought to be shot, she said.'
'She may have been reading, darling, that
Squirrels are only a kind of *rat.*'

'Goldfinches, Mother, owls and mice,
   Tom-tits and bunnies and jays—
Everything in my picture-books
   Will soon be gone, she says.'
'You see, my precious, so many creatures,
   Though exquisitely made,
Steal, or are dirty and dangerous,
   Or else they are bad for Trade.'

'I wonder, Mother, if when poor Noah
   Was alone in the rain and dark,

He can ever have thought what wicked things
 Were round him in the Ark. . . .
And are all children—like the rest—
Like me, as Nannie says, a pest?

'I woke last night from a dreadful dream
 Of a place—it was all of stone;
And dark. And the walls went up, and up—
 And oh, I was lost: alone!
I was *terrified,* Mother, and tried to call;
 But a gabble, like echoes, came back.
It will soon, I suppose, be bedtime again?
 And I hate lying there awake.'

'You mustn't, angel.' She glanced at the window—
 Smiled at the questioning mite.
'There's nothing to fear.' A wild bird scritched.
 The sun's last beam of light
Gilded the globe, reserved for Man,
 Preparing for the Night.

'DRY AUGUST BURNED'

Dry August burned. A harvest hare
Limp on the kitchen table lay,
Its fur blood-blubbered, eye astare,
While a small child that stood near by
Wept out her heart to see it there.

Sharp came the *clop* of hoofs, the clang
Of dangling chain, voices that rang.
Out like a leveret she ran,
To feast her glistening bird-clear eyes
On a team of field artillery
Gay, to manœuvres, thudding by.
Spur and gun and limber plate
Flashed in the sun. Alert, elate,
Noble horses, foam at lip,
Harness, stirrup, holster, whip,
She watched the sun-tanned soldiery,
Till dust-white hedge had hidden away—
Its din into a rumour thinned—
The laughing, jolting, wild array:
And then—the wonder and tumult gone—
Stood nibbling a green leaf, alone,
Her dark eyes, dreaming. . . . She turned, and ran,

Elf-like, into the house again.
The hare had vanished. . . . 'Mother,' she said,
Her tear-stained cheek now flushed with red,
'Please, may I go and see it skinned?'

'OF A SON'

A garish room—oil-lamped; a stove's warm blaze;
Gilt chairs drawn up to candles, and green baize:
The doctor hastened in—a moment stayed,
Watching the cards upon the table played—
Club, and sharp diamond, and heart, and spade.
And—still elated—he exclaimed, *'Parbleu,*
A thousand pardons, friends, for keeping you;
I feared I'd never see the lady through.
A boy, too! *Magnifique* the fight she made!
Ah, well, she's happy now!' Said one, ' "She"?—who?'
      'A woman called Landru.'

Gentle as flutter of dove's wing, the cards
Face downwards fell again; and fever-quick,
Topped by old Time and scythe, a small brass clock
In the brief hush of tongues resumed its tick.

ONE IN THE PUBLIC GALLERY

The Seraph scanned the murderer in the dock—
The motionless Judge, beneath the court-room clock,
The listening jury, warders, counsel, Clerk;
Ay, one and all who shared that deepening dark:
    And then, as I shunned to see,
He turned his burning eyes and looked at me.

SHADOW

*B*eware!—breathes the faint evening wind?
Omen—sighs dayspring's innocent air?
Stalks out from shadow, when drawn's the blind,
A warning Nothing, to shake the mind
    And touch the soul with care?—
    At midnight on thy stair?

Lurks there in every rose's sweet
A murderous whisper, *Fade must I?*
Mutters the vagrant in the street,
Edging his way with anxious feet—
    Thou too art hastening by.
    Drones on the carrion fly?

Oh, climb thou down from fool's disdain;
Stoop thy cold lips to rag and sore;
Kiss the gaunt cheek while yet remains
Life's blood in it. Ay, hearken; again!—
    Thou art the thief, the murderer,
    The outcast at thy door.

THE 'SATIRE'

The dying man on his pillow
   Turned slowly his head.
'Five years on my Satire on Man
   I spent,' he said.
'But, lying alone, I have mused
   On myself, of late!'

Smiling, he nodded; and glanced
   At the ash in the grate.

THE BRIDGE

With noble and strange devices Man hath spanned
River and torrent, raging in flood beneath;
But one more subtle than he ever planned
    Will exhaust my last faint breath:
A bridge, now nearing, I shall walk alone—
One pier on earth, the other in the unknown:
    And there, a viewless wraith—
Prince of the wreckage of the centuries,
Yet still past thought's fixed scrutiny, heart's surmise,
    And nought but a name, yet: Death.

SOLITUDE

Ghosts there must be with me in this old house,
Deepening its midnight as the clock beats on.
Whence else upwelled—strange, sweet, yet ominous—
That moment of happiness, and then was gone?

Nimbler than air-borne music, heart may call
A speechless message to the inward ear,
As secret even as that which then befell,
Yet nought that listening could make more clear.

Delicate, subtle senses, instant, fleet!—
But oh, how near the verge at which they fail!
In vain, self hearkens for the fall of feet
Soft as its own may be, beyond the pale.

INCANTATION

Vervain . . . basil . . . orison—
Whisper their syllablings till all meaning is gone,
And sound all vestige loses of mere word. . . .
'Tis then as if, in some far childhood heard,
A wild heart languished at the call of a bird,
Crying through ruinous windows, high and fair,
A secret incantation on the air:
A language lost; which, when its accents cease,
Breathes, voiceless, of a pre-Edenic peace.

A ROSE IN CANDLELIGHT

The oil in wild Aladdin's lamp
   A witching radiance shed;
But when its Genie absent was
   It languished, dull and dead.

Lo, now, the light that bathes this rose,
That wondrous red its cheek to give!
It breathes, 'We, too, a secret share;
Fleeting we are, however fair;
And only representative.'

DEFEAT

The way on high burned white beneath the sun,
Crag and gaunt pine stood stark in windless heat,
With sun-parched weeds its stones were over-run,
And he who had dared it, his long journey done,
Lay sunken in the slumber of defeat.

A raven low in the air, with stagnant eyes,
Poised in the instant of alighting gust,
Rent the thin silence with his hungry cries,
Voicing his greed o'er this far-scented prize,
Stiff in the invisible movement of the dust.

He lay, sharp-boned beneath his skin, half-nude,
His black hair tangled with a blackening red,
His gaze wide-staring in his solitude,
O'er which a bristling cloud of flies did brood,
In mumbling business with his heedless head.

Unfathomable drifts of space below,
Stretched, like grey glass, an infinite low sea,
Whereon a conflict of bright beams did flow,
In fiery splendour trembling to and fro—
The noon sun's angel-loosened archery.

And still on high, the way, a lean line, wound,
Wherefrom the raven had swooped down to eat,
To mortal eyes without an end, or bound,
Nor any creeping shadow to be found
To cool the sunken temples of defeat.

Defeat was scrawled upon each naked bone,
Defeat in the glazed vacancy of his eye,
Defeat his hand clutched in that waste of stone,
Defeat the bird yelped, and the flies' mazed drone
Lifted thanksgiving for defeat come by.

Lost in eternal rumination stare
Those darkened sockets of a dreamless head,
That cheek and jaw with the unpeopled air,
With smile immutable, unwearying, share
The subtle cogitations of the dead.

Yet, dwindling mark upon fate's viewless height,
For sign and token above the infinite sea,
'Neath the cold challenge of the all-circling night
Shall lie for witness in the Invisible's sight
The mockless victory that defeat may be.

AT EASE

Most wounds can Time repair;
But some are mortal, these:
For a broken heart there is no balm,
No cure for a heart at ease—

At ease, but cold as stone,
Though the intellect spin on,
And the feat and practised face may show
Nought of the life that is gone;

But smiles, as by habit taught;
And sighs, as by custom led;
And the soul within is safe from damnation,
Since it is dead.

AN ABANDONED CHURCH

Roofless and eyeless, weed-sodden, dank, old, cold—
Fickly the sunset glimmered through the rain,
Gilded the gravestones—faded out again;
A storm-cock shrilled its aeon-old refrain,
    Lambs bleated from their fold.

A ROSE IN WATER

A rose, in water, to its stem
Decoys a myriad beads of air;
And, lovely with the light on them,
Gives even its thorns their share.

NOT ONLY

Not only ruins their lichen have;
   Nor tombs alone, their moss.
Implacable Time, in markless grave,
   Turns what seemed gold to dross.

Yet—a mere ribbon for the hair,
   A broken toy, a faded flower
A passionate deathless grace may wear,
   Denied its passing hour.

EVENING

The little cirque, horizon-wide,
Of earth now swiftly draws away,
Though fulling moon aloft doth ride
Into the sun's perpetual day.

Little? It's all I have. For space
Than time itself's no less confined:
Its only being is what has place
At pin-point moment in the mind.

All history, knowledge, wisdom, power,
All man has said, or done, or made—
As transitory as a flower—
For me on this scant thread is stayed.

The all, the one; their better and worse,
Interdependent ever remain;
Each instant is my universe;
Which at a nod may fade again.

At the last slumber's nod, what then?

THE ASSIGNATION

Echoes of voices stilled may linger on
Until a lapse of utter quiet steal in;
As 'tis hushed daybreak—the dark night being gone—
That calls small birds their matins to begin. . . .

Felled with such sickness I had lain that life
Nightmare's phantasmagoria seemed to be.
Alas, poor body, racked with woe and strife,
Its very weakness set my spirit free.

Wondrous the regions then through which I strayed,
Spectre invisible as the wind and air,
Regions that midnight fantasy had made,
And clear cold consciousness can seldom share.

But of these wanderings one remembered best
Nothing exotic showed—no moon-drenched vale,
Where in profound ravines dark forests rest,
The wild-voiced cataracts their nightingale;

But only a sloping meadow, rimed with frost;
Bleak pollard willows, and a frozen brook,
All tinkle of its waters hushed and lost,
Its sword-sharp rushes by the wind forsook:

An icy-still, grey-heavened, vacant scene,
With whin and marron hummocked, and flowerless gorse . . .
And in that starven upland's winter green,
Stood grazing in the silence a white horse.

No marvel of beauty, or strangeness, or fable, this—
Una—la Belle Dame—hero—or god might ride;
Worn, aged with time and toil, and now at peace,
It cropped earth's sweetmeats on the stark hill's side.

Spellbound, I watched it—hueless mane and tail
Like wraith of foam upon an un-named sea;
Until, as if at mute and inward hail,
It raised its gentle head and looked at me—

Eyes blue as speedwell, tranquil, morning-fair:
It was as if for aeons these and I
Had planned this mystic assignation there,
In this lone waste, beneath that wintry sky . .

Strange is man's soul, which solace thus can win,
When the poor body lies at woe's extreme—
Yea, even where the shades of death begin—
In secret symbol, and painted by a dream!

CLAVICHORD

Hearken! Tiny, clear, discrete:
The listener within deems solely his,
    A music so remote and sweet
It all but lovely as silence is.

MEMORY

Ah, Memory—that strange deceiver!
Who can trust her?   How believe her—
While she hoards with equal care
The poor and trivial, rich and rare;
Yet flings away, as wantonly,
Grave fact and loveliest fantasy?

When I call her—need her most,
Lo, she's in hiding, or is lost!
Or, capricious as the wind,
Brings stalks—and leaves the flowers behind.
Of all existence—as I live—
She can no more than moments give.
Thousands of dew-clear dusks in Spring
Were mine, time gone, to wander in,
But of their fragrance, music, peace,
What now is left my heart to bless?—
Oases in a wilderness!
Nor could her tongue tell o'er the tale
Even of one June nightingale.
And what of the strange world that teems—
Where brooding Hypnos reigns—with dreams?
Twenty years in sleep I have spent—
Horror, delight, grief, wonderment;

Through what wild wizard scenes lured on!
Where are they? . . . In oblivion.
Told she her all, 'twould reach an end
Ere nodded off the drowsiest friend!

She has, it's true, a sovereign skill
A wounded heart to salve and heal;
Can lullaby to sorrow sing;
Shed balm on grief and suffering;
And guard with unremitting care
Secrets that we alone can share.
Ay, so bewitched her amber is
'Twill keep enshrined the tiniest flies—
Instants of childhood, fresh as when
My virgin sense perceived them then—
Daisy or rainbow, a look, a kiss,
As safe as if Eternity's;
And can, with probe as keen, restore
Some fear, or woe, when I was four.
Fleeter than Nereid, plummet-deep,
Enticed by some long-sunken ship,
She, siren-wise, laughs out to see
The treasure she retrieves for me—
Gold foundered when I was a boy,
Now cleansed by Time from all alloy.
And think what priceless boons I owe
Her whimsical punctilio!

Nothing would recognition bring
Should she forsake me.   Everything
I will, or want, or plan, or say
Were past conceiving, she away.
Only her exquisite vigilance
Enables me to walk, sing, dance.
Tree and bird would name-less pine
Did she the twain refuse to entwine.
And where, sad dunce, if me she shun,
My A B C? my twice times one?
Fancy her nurseling is; and thought
Can solely in her toils be caught.
Ev'n who and where and what I am
Await her whisper to proclaim.

If only—what the infinite loss!—
I had helped her sever gold from dross!
Since now she is—for better or worse—
The relics of my Universe.
But, ah, how scant a heed she pays
To much well-meaning Conscience says!
And good intentions?   Alas for them!
They are left to languish on the stem.
The mort of promises idly made—
Where now their husks, the fickle jade?
Where, too, the jilt so gaily resigned
To out-of-sight being out-of-mind?

And, Love?—I would my heart and she
Were more attuned to constancy!

Musing, she sits, at ease, in peace,
Unchanged by age or time's caprice,
And quietly cons again with me
Some well-loved book of poetry,
Her furtive finger putting by,
With a faint smile, or fainter sigh,
The withered flowers that mark a place
Once over-welled with grief or grace.
Yes, and, as though the wanton tried
Once bitter pangs to gloss, or hide,
She stills a voice fall'n harsh and hoarse
With sudden ill-concealed remorse.
I scan the sphinx-like face, and ask
What still lies hid beneath that mask?—
The sins, the woes, the perfidy—
O murderous taciturnity!
I am the *all* I have ever been,
Why gild the cage thou keep'st me in?
Sweet, sweet, she mocks me, the siren; and then
Its very bars shine bright again.

Yet, of my life, from first to last,
This wayward mistress of the Past—
Soundless foot, and tarn-dark eyes—
Keeps safe for me what most I prize.

The sage may to the Future give
Their *Now,* however fugitive;
Mine savours less of rue and myrrh
When spent, in solitude, with her;
When, kingfisher, on leafy spray,
I while the sunshine hours away
In tranquil joy—as in a dream—
Not of its fish, but of the stream;
Whose gliding waters then reflect
Serener skies, in retrospect,
And flowers, ev'n fairer to the eye
Than those of actuality.

And with what grace she has dealt with me—
What patience, insight, sorcery!
Why, every single word here writ
Was hers, till she surrendered it;
And where, without her—I?   For lo,
When she is gone I too must go.

THE MOMENT

O Time—the heedless child you are!
A daisy, the most distant star
Fall to your toying scimitar.
And I? And this loved face? We too
Are things but of a moment. True:
But then, poor youngling, so are you!

Dream on! In your small company
We are contented merely to be—
Yes, even to Eternity.

FAINT MUSIC

The meteor's arc of quiet; a voiceless rain;
The mist's mute communing with a stagnant moat;
The sigh of a flower that has neglected lain;
    That bell's unuttered note:

A hidden self rebels, its slumber broken;
Love secret as crystal forms within the womb;
The heart may as faithfully beat, the vow unspoken;
    All sounds to silence come.

WAITING

'Waiting to . . .'
'Who is?'
'We are . . .
Was that the night-owl's cry?'
'I heard not. But see! the evening star;
And listen!—the ocean's solacing sigh.'
'You mean the surf at the harbour bar?'
'What did you say?'
'Oh, "waiting." '
' "Waiting?"—
Waiting what for?'
'To die.'

EUPHRASY

Hope, wreathed with roses,
Led sand-blind Despair
To a clear babbling wellspring
And laved his eyes there—
Dark with long brooding
In dungeon-like keep—
Hope laved his eyes,
And he fell fast asleep.

He fell fast asleep
By the willows green-grey,
While the child on his pipes
Piped twilight away.
So that when he awoke
The skies were outspread
With a powder of stars
Strewn in myriads o'erhead.

And Despair lifted up
His gaunt cavernous face;
He said, 'I see Suns
Like wild beacons, in space;
I cannot endure
The blaze, dazzle, flare!'

But the child—he saw only
Faint stars glinting there.

And he flung back his head
With laughter at sight
Of that lantern-jawed face
Dazed with fear at the Night.
And he counselled Despair
Some sly shift to devise
Lest daybreak brought blindness—
Again—to his eyes.

And he his young brows
Sprinkled cold in the brook
For the magic of starshine
Which them had forsook.

THE STRATAGEM

Here's the cave where Sorrow dwells
Weeping in his courts of yew!
Foot then lightly in these dells,
Let not plash one drop of dew;
Bring your chains of pimpernels,
Bring your silvery honeydew.

Lay your nets deliciously,
Set the bait in that sweet beam—
One grey tear to lure him by
When he wakens from his dream,
And the breath of a faint sigh,
That shall ev'n less be than seem.

Hide you, hide you, not a note,
From the little birds you are!
Let not the least laughter float
Near or far, near or far!
See he wakens! scare him not—
Wild with weeping as a star.

Hie away, ah, hie away!
Woe is all, see, how the sun
Ruddies through his filmy grey,

Turns to light the dreaming one—
Mist and dew of a Spring day
Trembling a night-nothing on.

Fold your nets and mew your bait!
Come, sweet spirits, how shall we
Watch, and never ending, wait
For a wraith of transiency?
Fly ere yet the day grow late,
Else we too grow shadowy!

HOMESICK

O homesick, brood no more!
Lovely that sky; haunted the wandering wind;
Strange the dark breakers beating on the shore
That never rest, nor any respite find,
Yet ever call to the lone ghost in thee,
'Where is thy peace, where thy tranquillity?'

Only a wasting fire
Is this remembrance, cheating day and night
With vain and unassuageable desire,
And fleeting phantom pictures of delight.
And yet, O sleep—friend of my body—be
Friend to the soul also that thirsts for thee!

OUT OF BOUNDS

Why covet what eye cannot see;
  Or earthly longing know?
Decoyed by cheating fantasy—
  This restless ranging to and fro?

Would wildlier sing dark's nightingale
  Where Hera's golden apples grow?
Would lovelier be the swallow's flight
In wastes of wild auroral night,
  Wondrous with falling snow?

NIGHT

That shining moon—watched by that one faint star:
Sure now am I, beyond the fear of change,
The lovely in life is the familiar,
And only the lovelier for continuing strange.

PEACE

Night is o'er England, and the winds are still;
Jasmine and honeysuckle steep the air;
Softly the stars that are all Europe's fill
Her heaven-wide dark with radiancy fair;
That shadowed moon now waxing in the west
Stirs not a rumour in her tranquil seas;
Mysterious sleep has lulled her heart to rest,
Deep even as theirs beneath her churchyard trees.

Secure, serene; dumb now the night-hawk's threat;
The guns' low thunder drumming o'er the tide;
The anguish pulsing in her stricken side. . . .
All is at peace. . . . But, never, heart, forget:
For this her youngest, best, and bravest died,
These bright dews once were mixed with bloody sweat.

THE WIDOW

Grief now hath pacified her face;
Even hope might share so still a place.
Yet, if—in silence of her heart—
A memoried voice or footstep start,
Or a chance word of ecstasy
Cry through dim-cloistered memory,
Into her eyes her soul will steal
To gaze on the irrevocable—
As if death had not power to keep
One, who had loved her long, so long asleep.

Now all things lovely she looks on
Wear the mute aspect of oblivion;
And all things silent seem to be
Richer than any melody.
Her narrow hands, like birds that make
A nest for some old instinct's sake,
Have hollowed a refuge for her face—
A narrow and a darkened place—
Where, far from the world's light, she may
See clearer what is passed away:
And only little children know
Through what dark half-closed gates her smile may go.

THE LAST CHAPTER

I am living more alone now than I did;
This life tends inward, as the body ages;
And what is left of its strange book to read
Quickens in interest with the last few pages.

Problems abound. Its authorship? A sequel?
Its hero-villain, whose ways so little mend?
The plot? still dark. The style? a shade unequal.
And what of the dénouement? And, the end?

No, no, have done! Lay the thumbed thing aside;
Forget its horrors, folly, incitements, lies;
In silence and in solitude abide,
And con what yet may bless your inward eyes.

Pace, still, for pace with you, companion goes,
Though now, through dulled and inattentive ear,
No more—as when a child's—your sick heart knows
His infinite energy and beauty near.

His, too, a World, though viewless save in glimpse;
He, too, a book of imagery bears;
And as your halting foot beside him limps,
Mark you whose badge and livery he wears.

COURAGE

O heart, hold thee secure
In this blind hour of stress,
Live on, love on, endure,
Uncowed, though comfortless.

Life's still the wondrous thing
It seemed in bygone peace,
Though woe now jar the string,
And all its music cease.

Even if thine own self have
No haven for defence;
Stand not the unshaken brave
To give thee confidence?

Worse than all worst 'twould be,
If thou, who art thine all,
Shatter ev'n their reality
    In thy poor fall!

MARTINS: SEPTEMBER

At secret daybreak they had met—
　　Chill mist beneath the welling light
Screening the marshes green and wet—
　　An ardent legion wild for flight.

Each preened and sleeked an arrowlike wing;
　　Their eager throats with lapsing cries
Praising whatever fate might bring—
　　Cold wave, or Africa's paradise.

Unventured, trackless leagues of air,
　　England's sweet summer narrowing on,
Her lovely pastures: nought their care—
　　Only this ardour to be gone.

A tiny, elflike, ecstatic host . . .
　　And 'neath them, on the highway's crust,
Like some small mute belated ghost,
　　A sparrow pecking in the dust.

SUNRISE

Bliss it is at break of day
To watch the night-mists thin away:
Like wraiths, of light distilled, they seem—
Phantoms of beauty from a forgotten dream.

As if to a new world new-bidden,
The risen sun shines through the gates of heaven;
And, since the meagrest face with joy may shine,
His glory greets the candle-flame in mine.

THE DREAMER

The woods were still. No breath of air
   Stirred in leaf or brake.
Cold hung the rose, unearthly fair;
   The nightingale, awake,
In rusted coverts of the may
   Shook out his bosom's down;
Alone, upon her starry way,
   The moon, to fulness grown,
Moved, shining, through her misty meads;
   And, roofless from the dew,
Knelt way-worn Love, with idle beads,
    And dreamed of you.

SALLIE'S MUSICAL BOX

Once it made music, tiny, frail, yet sweet—
Bead-note of bird where earth and elfland meet.
Now its thin tinkling stirs no more, since she
Whose toy it was, has gone; and taken the key.

A PORTRAIT

A solemn plain-faced child stands gazing there,
Her small hand resting on a purple chair.
Her stone-grey waisted gown is looped with black;
Linked chain and star encircle a slender neck;
Knots of bright red deck wrist, breast, flaxen hair;
Shoulder to waist falls band of lettered gold:
Round-eyed, she watches me—this eight-year-old,
The ghost of her father in her placid stare.

Darkness beyond.   A moment she and I
Engage in some abstruse small colloquy—
On time, art, beauty, life, mortality!
But of one secret not a hint creeps out—
What grave Velasquez talked to her about;
And from that shadow not a clapper cries
Where now the fowler weaves his subtleties.

BRUEGHEL'S WINTER

Jagg'd mountain peaks and skies ice-green
Wall in the wild, cold scene below.
Churches, farms, bare copse, the sea
In freezing quiet of winter show;
Where ink-black shapes on fields in flood
Curling, skating, and sliding go.
To left, a gabled tavern; a blaze;
Peasants; a watching child; and lo,
Muffled, mute—beneath naked trees
In sharp perspective set a-row—
Trudge huntsmen, sinister spears aslant,
Dogs snuffling behind them in the snow;
And arrowlike, lean, athwart the air
    Swoops into space a crow.

But flame, nor ice, nor piercing rock,
Nor silence, as of a frozen sea,
Nor that slant inward infinite line
Of signboard, bird, and hill, and tree,
Give more than subtle hint of him
Who squandered here life's mystery.

O CHILDISH MIND!

O childish mind!—last night to rapture won
In marvel of wild Orion; now to sink
Earthward; and by the flames of a dwarf sun
Find a like happiness in a single pink!

UNFORESEEN

Darkness had fallen. I opened the door:
And lo, a stranger in the empty room—
A marvel of moonlight upon wall and floor . . .
The quiet of mercy? Or the hush of doom?

TWICE LOVELY

Chalk-white, light dazzled on the stone,
And there a weed, a finger high,
Bowed its silvery head with every
Breath of wind that faltered by.

Twice lovely thing! For when there drifted
A cloud across the radiant sun,
Not only that had it forsaken,
Its tiny shadow too was gone.

THE DAISY

Oh, saw I there—
Under bleak shadow of a towering wall,
From its great height let fall,
Dense-historied, and, echoing from its stone,
Ruinous, mossed, and lone,
The crying fowls of the air—
Set in a smooth, cool flood of agelong green,
Reared up on inch-high stalk, to see, be seen,
A pygmy daisy, with a silver face,
Shining in that dark place.

FOREBODING

The sycamore, by the heap of dead
   Summer's last flowers that rot below,
Will suddenly in the stillness shed
   A cockled leaf from a bud-tight bough:
So ghostlike the sound that I turn my head
As if at a whisper—at something said;
   'What! And still happy? Thou!'

That is this captious phantom's way—
   Omens, monitions, hints of fate,
On a quiet, air-sweet October day
   Of beauty past estimate!
Is it age; or conscience; or mind now fey
At a world from love so far astray
   That can only falter, 'Wait'?

WHICH?

'What did you say?'
'I? Nothing.' 'No? . . .
What was that sound?'
'When?'
'Then.'
'I do not know.'
'Whose eyes were those on us?'
'Where?'
'There.'
'No eyes I saw.'
'Speech, footfall, presence—how cold the night may be!'
'Phantom or fantasy, it's all one to *me*.'

THE CHERRY TREES

Under pure skies of April blue I stood,
Where in wild beauty cherries were in blow;
And, as sweet fancy willed, see there I could
Boughs thick with blossom, or inch-deep in snow.

THE WINDOW

Sunlit, the lashes fringe the half-closed eyes
With hues no bow excels that spans the skies;
As magical the meteor's flight o'erhead,
And daybreak shimmering on a spider's thread.

Thou starry Universe—whose breadth, depth, height
Contracts to such strait entry as mere sight!

THE DOVE

How often, these hours, have I heard the monotonous crool
   of a dove—
Voice, low, insistent, obscure, since its nest it has hid in a
   grove—
Flowers of the linden wherethrough the hosts of the honey-
   bees rove.

And I have been busily idle: no problems; nothing to prove;
No urgent foreboding; but only life's shallow habitual
   groove:
Then why, if I pause to listen, should the languageless note
   of a dove
So dark with disquietude seem?   And what is it sorrow-
   ing of?

SWALLOWS FLOWN

Whence comes that small continuous silence
   Haunting the livelong day?—
This void, where a sweetness, so seldom heeded,
   Once ravished my heart away?
As if a loved one, too little valued,
   Had vanished—could not stay?

A QUEEN WASP

Why rouse from thy long winter sleep?
And sound that witchcraft drone in air?
The frost-bound hours of darkness creep,
    The night is cold, and bare

Of all that gave thee power to rear
Thy myriad Amazonian host.
All, all are dust. I only, here;
    And thou—untimely ghost!—

Prowling, black-orbed, disconsolate,
Questing antennae, quivering wing,
Unwitting of the mortal fate
    A human thought might bring

To the mute marvels in thy womb,
Tarrying only summer's heat
To breed a Babylon from the tomb—
    As wondrous and exquisite!

Still, now. Thou'rt safe and hidden again;
Thy sombre, astonished piping done . . .
And I, with the hosts that flock the brain,
    Back to my self am gone.

A HARE

Eyes that glass fear, though fear on furtive foot
    Track thee, in slumber bound;
Ears that whist danger, though the wind sigh not,
    Nor Echo list a sound;
Heart—oh, what hazard must thy wild life be,
With sapient Man for thy cold enemy!

Fleet Scatterbrains, thou hast thine hours of peace
    In pastures April-green,
Where the shrill skylark's raptures never cease,
And the clear dew englobes the white moon's beam.
All happiness God gave thee, albeit thy foe
Roves Eden, as did his Satan, long ago.

A DREAM

Idle I sat—my book upon my knee,
The Tyro's Outline of Biology.
Drowsy the hour: and wits began to roam
Far, far from gene, as far from chromosome.
Sweet sleep stole over me. . . .

                    A valley in Spring!—
Wherein a river of water crystal clear
In rarer beauty imaged all things near—
Green grass, and leaf; lithe leopard, swift gazelle—
Gihon? Euphrates? No, I could not tell,
But knew it was Eden by the asphodel,
The painted birds, the songs I heard them sing.

There, where heaven's sunbeams with earth's shade inwove,
This side a slumber-solemn cedar grove,
A clear green twilight underneath a tree—
Of Life? Of Knowledge? it was strange to me—
Two mortals sat: a sage, dome-headed, grey,
Who looked a child, albeit in age astray—
Talking, it seemed, his very heart away;
And one even lovelier than woods in May.

She, as if poesy haunted all he said—
Eyes blue as chicory flower, and braided head—

· 72 ·

Showed silent as snow against the tender grass,
For naked she as Aphrodite was.
And, at her shoulder, mid its coils near by,
A subtle Serpent couched, with lidless eye,
Which, its tongue flickering, else motionlessly,
Raised its rune-blazoned head, and gazed at me.

Whereat, although it harmless seemed, I woke;
My dream-cleansed eyes now fixed upon my book;
Nor could by any stealth I entry win
Into that paradisal scene again—
Fruit so much sweeter to a childish love
Than any knowledge I had vestige of.

Mingled the moonlight with daylight—the last in the narrowing West;

Silence of nightfall lay over the shallowing valleys at rest
In the Earth's green breast:

Yet a small multitudinous singing, a lully of voices of birds,

Unseen in the vague shelving hollows, welled up with my questioning words:

All Dorsetshire's larks for connivance of sweetness seemed trysting to greet

Him in whose songs the bodings of raven and nightingale meet.

Stooping and smiling, he questioned, 'No birdnotes myself do I hear?

Perhaps 'twas the talk of chance farers, abroad in the hush with us here—
In the dusk-light clear?'

And there peered from his eyes, as I listened, a concourse of women and men,

Whom his words had made living, long-suffering—they flocked to remembrance again;

'O Master,' I cried in my heart, 'lorn thy tidings, grievous thy song;

Yet thine, too, this solacing music, as we earthfolk stumble along.'

ROOKS IN OCTOBER

They sweep up, crying, riding the wind,
    Ashen on blue outspread—
Gilt-lustred wing, sharp light-glazed beak,
    And low flat ravenous head.

Claws dangling, down they softly swoop
    Out of the eastern sun
Into the yellowing green-leaved boughs—
    Their morning feast begun.

Clasping a twig that even a linnet
    Might bend in song, they clip
Pat from the stalked embossed green cup
    Its fruitage bitter-ripe.

Oh, what divine far hours their beauty
    Of old for me beguiled,
When—acorn, oak, untarnished heavens—
    I watched them as a child!

THE CAGE

Thou angel face!—like a small exquisite cage,
     Such as some old Chinese
Once spent his love and skill on—youth to age,
In hope its destined prisoner to please;
And then had empty left; since he had heard
What death would do in setting free the bird.

QUIET

Mutely the mole toils on;
The worm in silk cocoon
Stealthy as spider spins,
  As glides the moon.
But listen where envy peers beneath half-closed lid;
Where peeping vanity lurks; where pride lies hid;
And peace beyond telling share with the light-stilled eye,
When only the image of the loved one's nigh.

THE OLD SUMMERHOUSE

This blue-washed, old, thatched summerhouse—
Paint scaling, and fading from its walls—
How often from its hingeless door
I have watched—dead leaf, like the ghost of a mouse,
Rasping the worn brick floor—
The snows of the weir descending below,
And their thunderous waterfall.

Fall—fall: dark, garrulous rumour,
Until I could listen no more.
Could listen no more—for beauty with sorrow
Is a burden hard to be borne:
The evening light on the foam, and the swans, there;
That music, remote, forlorn.

THE CAPTIVE

When gloaming droops
To the raven's croak,
And the nightjar churs
From his time-gnarled oak
In the thunder-stricken wood:

When the drear dark waters
'Neath sallows hoar
Shake the veils of night
With their hollow roar,
Plunging deep in flood;

Spectral, wan
From unquiet rest,
A phantom walks
With anguished breast,
Doomed to love's solitude.

Her footstep is leaf-like,
Light as air,
Her raiment scarce stirs
The gossamer.
While from shadowy hood

In the wood-light pale
Her dream-ridden eyes,
Without sorrow or tear,
Speculation, surmise,
Wildly, insanely brood.

AN INTERLUDE

A small brook gushed on stones hard by,
Waste-lorn it babbled; alone was I,
Dawn's ever-changing alchemy
  Low in the eastern sky.

Ghost that I was, by dream waylaid,
Benighted, and yet unafraid,
I sat, in those brief hours, long-lost,
  And communed with the sea.

Faint, o'er its shingly murmuring,
The secret songs I had hoped to sing—
When I on earth was sojourning—
Of which poor words, alas, can bring
Only a deadened echoing
  Of what they meant to me—
Rose in my throat; and poured their dew—
A hymn of praise—my being through;
Shed peace on a mind that never knew
  Peace in that mind could be.

Only a soundless voice was I,
Yet sweeter that than man can hear
When, latticed in by moonbeams clear,

The bird of darkness to its fere
    Tells out love's mystery.

No listener there—a dream; but ne'er
Sang happier heart in heaven fair
    To lyre or psaltery. . . .

Oh, futile vanity to mourn
What the day's waking leaves forlorn!
Doth not earth's strange and lovely mean
Only, 'Come, see, O son of man,
All that you hope, the nought you can,
    The glory that might have been?'

A PRAYER

When with day's woes night haunts wake-weary eyes,
How deep a blessing from the heart may rise
On the happy, the beautiful, the good, the wise.

The poor, the outcast, knave, child, stranger, fool—
Need no commending to the merciful;
But, in a world grieved, ugly, wicked, or dull,

Who could the starry influence surmise—
What praises ardent enough could prayer devise
For the happy, the beautiful, the good, the wise?

'HERE SLEEPS'

Here sleeps, past earth's awakening,
A woman, true and pretty;
Who was herself in everything—
Tender, and grave, and witty.
Her lightest turn of foot, hand, head,
Was way of wind with water;
So with her thoughts and all she said—
It seemed her heart had taught her.
O thou most dear and loving soul,
Think not I shall forget thee;
Nor take amiss what here is writ
For those who never met thee!

THE LAST ARROW

There came a boy,
Full quiver on his back—
Tapped at my door ajar.

'No, no, my child,' said I,
'I nothing lack;
And see!—the evening star!'

Finger on string,
His dangerous eyes
Gazed boldly into mine:

'Know thou my mother
An Immortal is!
Guard thee, and hope resign!'

'But patience,' I pleaded,
Pointing to a shelf,
Where rusting arrows lay.

'All these, times gone,
You squandered on myself,
Why come—so late, to-day?'

These words scarce uttered,
I discerned a Shade
Shadow till then had hid;

Clang went that bowstring,
And past wit to evade,
Into my bosom slid

His final dart.
He shook his rascal head,
Its curls by the lamp-shine gilt:

'Thank thou the Gods!
Here's One, I vow,' he said,
'Not even thee shall jilt.'

AWAY

There is no sorrow
Time heals never;
No loss, betrayal,
Beyond repair.
Balm for the soul, then,
Though grave shall sever
Lover from loved
And all they share;
See, the sweet sun shines,
The shower is over,
Flowers preen their beauty,
The day how fair!

Brood not too closely
On love, or duty;
Friends long forgotten
May wait you where
Life with death
Brings all to an issue;
None will long mourn for you,
Pray for you, miss you,
Your place left vacant,
You not there.

'OH, WHY?'

Oh, why make such ado—
This fretful care and trouble?
The sun in noonday's blue
Pours radiance on earth's bubble.
What though the heart-strings crack,
And sorrow bid thee languish,
Dew falls; the night comes back;
Sleep, and forget thine anguish.
Oh, why in shadow haunt?
Shines not the evening flower?
Hark, how the sweet birds chaunt,
The lovely light their bower.
Water her music makes,
Lulling even these to slumber;
And only dead of darkness wakes
Stars without number.

THE LOOKING-GLASS

'Nothing is so sure that it
May not in a moment flit:
Quench the candle, gone are all
The wavering shadows on the wall.
Eros, like Time, is winged. And, why?
To warn us, dear, he too can fly.
Watch, now, your bright image here
In this water, calm and fair—
Those clear brown eyes, that dark brown hair.
See, I fling a pebble in;
What distortions now begin!
Refluent ripples sweep and sway,
Chasing all I love away.
But, imagine a strange glass
Which, to gaze, gave back, alas,
Nothing but a crystal wall,
And else, no hint of you at all:
No rose on cheek, no red on lip,
No trace of beauty's workmanship.
That, my dear, for me, for you,
Precisely is what life might do.
Might, I say. . . . Oh, then, how sweet
Is it by this stream to sit,

And in its molten mirror see
All that is now reality:
The interlacing boughs, the sun's
Tiny host of flickering moons,
That rainbow kingfisher, and these
Demure, minute anemones—
Cherubim, in heaven's blue,
Leaning their wizard faces too—
Lost in delight at seeing *you*.'

SNOW

This meal-white snow—
Oh, look at the bright fields!
What crystal manna
Death-cold winter yields!

Falling from heavens
Earth knows little of,
Yet mantling it
As with a flawless love—

A shining cloak—
It to the naked gives,
Wooing all sorrow
From the soul it shrives.

Adam no calmer vales
Than these descried;
Leda a shadow were
This white beside.

Water stays still for wonder;
Herb and flower,
Else starved with cold,
In warmth and darkness cower.

Miracle, far and near,
That starry flake
Can of its myriads
Such wide pastures make,

For sun to colour,
And for moon to wan,
And day's vast vault of blue
To arch upon!

A marvel of light,
Whose verge of radiance seems
Frontier of paradise,
The bourne of dreams.

O tranquil, silent, cold—
Such loveliness to see:
The heart sighs answer,
Benedicite!